About the Author

A thinker, dreamer who finds equal interest in spirituality, knowing the Self and at the same time knowing the stars, galaxies and the universe and perhaps the ultimate link between all of this. A pharmacist, daughter, sister, wife and now a mother. Born and raised in India but I found my spirituality in the west in my late 20s residing in America.

The Doer

Rekha Nair

The Doer

Olympia Publishers
London

www.olympiapublishers.com
OLYMPIA PAPERBACK EDITION

Copyright © Rekha Nair 2024

The right of Rekha Nair to be identified as author of
this work has been asserted in accordance with sections 77 and 78 of
the Copyright, Designs and Patents Act 1988.

All Rights Reserved

No reproduction, copy or transmission of this publication
may be made without written permission.
No paragraph of this publication may be reproduced,
copied or transmitted save with the written permission of the publisher,
or in accordance with the provisions
of the Copyright Act 1956 (as amended).

Any person who commits any unauthorised act in relation to
this publication may be liable to criminal
prosecution and civil claims for damage.

A CIP catalogue record for this title is
available from the British Library.

ISBN: 978-1-80439-495-3

This book has a recollection of actual events from the life of the author.
All persons within are actual individuals.

First Published in 2024

Olympia Publishers
Tallis House
2 Tallis Street
London
EC4Y 0AB

Printed in Great Britain

Dedication

I dedicate this book to every person who has walked into my life. Some who left and some who stayed. All of you have touched me and helped me grow.

Acknowledgements

Thank you to this life that has given me the environment and circumstances to create this writing. Thank you to my husband, Tushar for understanding my freedom and letting me evolve. Thank you to all my family and friends for being my pillar of support always. Thank you, Kabir, for choosing me as you mother and changing my life forever.

This book is my journey to the Self. The Doer is about what is out there in our everyday lives, that's the biggest teacher, influencer and inspiration. A quest to the find how desires, intentions and aspirations sprout in us. Who brings them in our hearts and what is its purpose? The Doer touches upon the subject of what letting go truly means. It's an approach in explaining what is in control and what is not. We often complicate spirituality with ideas, dogmas, dos and don'ts. I believe that everything we do is already spiritual. Because at every step it is unveiling something about this life and why we are here. The plan is already in place for you, to take you where you are destined to arrive. The rights and wrongs are just a matter of our progress and how we interpret things. As we start progressing in life, our interpretations change, and life seems to make more sense. And through this journey of unveiling, we find the connection between everything that exists and how everyone is leading a journey to the Self, the source, the Doer.

INTRODUCTION

1. Have we forgotten?
2. What have we forgotten?
3. What is Love?
4. What is the nature of the soul?
5. God is?
6. Why is freedom important?
7. What is the relevance of cyclic events and things that exist in pairs?
8. What is the toughest thing to overcome?
9. What is a choice, and does it exist?
10. What does connecting mean?
11. What do you value the most?
12. You rather experience and know or do you want to know and then experience. Also, why?

The Doer

Who is doing the work? Is it the thoughts I am having? Is it my intentions? Or is it my desires, needs or actions, that's doing the work? Who is doing the work...?

If it is not me, then who is it? And how much does it do? Is 80% done already and I (as in my ego) need to finish the 20%? This is an important question for me. Being responsible, decisive, thoughtful, aware ...all that comes to existence so my ego can follow the right path. An important understanding here is that my ego is somewhere, partly the doer. And since it's the doer, it needs to be all that, to be on the "right path". But is it though? If everything is destined, then why do we stress? Why do we fear? Why do we feel lost?

A simple answer to this complicated thought is - because the ego thinks it's the doer. Ego that believes to be in control. Even if it's at a minuscule level. And when the ego thinks it's in control, it has a certain expectation of the inputs and outputs it gives and takes. And when things don't happen that way, because it is the act of a cosmic energy that determines the input and output and not the ego, the ego undergoes stress. The human is in stress. The human starts to think it's not in control. And a human who thinks is not in control often feels defeated, stressed, demotivated.

So, you obviously must let go of something for the ego to understand. And what it is to let go is so subtle. One may ask, should we stop thinking? Should we stop doing anything? Should we withdraw from performing any actions? And we are again caught in the same puzzle. We are caught because the thought is that there is something we need to do to lead a happy, peaceful, fulfilled life. But, what we are to lead, how we are to lead comes to life with your own life. And as you experience the ride, the awareness gets fine-tuned with your progress in the journey of life. And that's exactly what's hard to do. Because the ego wants to be in control, on some level. We like to reward and punish ourselves for what's happening in our lives. Many don't really sit and analyze if what happened, really happened because of their ego 'I' or if there was a higher hand of something that's beyond us. Once you start observing and asking this question in everything, one will start feeling a liberation like never before. It's the liberation from ego. The more you realize the higher hand, the weaker the ego gets and the more liberated one feels.

To many, the idea of not being the Doer translates to laziness. Its limiting - not taking accountability of one's own life. Understand who is the Doer and who is not but more importantly understand who you are. Are you the ego or are you beyond ego? How do we know the difference? The easiest way to test if you are the ego is by letting go of the ego and see how you feel. Do you feel like you are dying, or do you feel liberated at some level? This might be a challenging exercise for those who have a high ego quotient. They may have to repeat the exercise multiple times to see how they really feel ultimately. But again, letting go of ego is no less of an art. There is a symphony to it. There is a rhythm to it. There is a way to it. There is a story to it. Letting go of ego doesn't happen in a moment. You are led to that moment. And when you realize everything that led you to that moment, that's when you truly realize how you feel when you let go of that ego. The very idea that you are letting go of something, tells you, you are not it. You are something that the ego was attached to. You are more than the ego. When you let go of ego, you let go of sense of effort, action and result. Not just for yourself but also for others. Sense of judgement fades away. You now not only start seeing your path, but you also see the path of others. You recognize their stops, bumps, roadblocks. Empathy inevitably seeps in but more importantly, you stop trying to fix things because you simply know the arrow is always pointing forward and everything that needs to take them forward is already in place. You may or may not be used as an instrument.

Whatever happens, happened and will happen is not in the control of the ego. But, for this to be true, this truth should be applicable in anything and everything. Not just on an impactful event. That's the thing about mundane events. It's hard to find the ultimate source when it comes to mundane things. But, if you sit with a centered mind, you will get to the source of everything. Anything and everything happening in life, be it a petal falling, a new leaf growing or moving or changing or not changing .... Everything is destined. And so is liberation from the illusion of ego. Liberation is a state that everyone will experience. And if one doesn't now, it's because there are on the path of progress to get there. It's a part of the evolution of our consciousness.

The very fact that my birth happened before my intentions did, gives me an understanding that I am here for a reason that's above my intentions also. The purpose was set, and I was born. I was born with various tools like intentions, desires, failures and success to achieve the purpose I am here for. So are all of us. Every experience just removes a layer off of the onion. Unveiling what's underneath. So, the very moment you are in - good, bad, ugly, beautiful, confusing, uncertain, challenging, hurtful .... is exactly where you are meant to be. No one is punishing you. You are only getting taught. And sometimes you learn easy and other times you learn the hard way.

A while ago my life went through a churning process. As I was coming out of a difficult phase, the awareness started shifting. It began with a phase of freeze. Time froze for me momentarily. My desires wanted to move forward faster than my heartbeat, but I felt something strongly holding me back, asking me to be still and observe. Initially it felt like a strange inhibition but soon it revealed something profound. It felt like I had taken my hand out of flowing water. Water kept flowing but my hand couldn't feel the motion. It took me a minute, but I finally got it. My hand really didn't have a role in the flow of water, but it was the water that gave me the sense of flow. It wasn't my desires taking me forward but an underlying current of purpose that was the driving force. It gave me an understanding that it didn't matter. What desires you have doesn't matter but it's the purpose that lies underneath the desire, that makes all the difference. A purpose for you in the Doer. Life is nothing but fine tuning to this purpose. Working through desires, intentions, actions as a medium to carry out the purpose it has in you. Somewhere it showed me how much I wasn't in control. Something higher was.

This was only the beginning of a very long journey I had to undertake towards the Self. This was the beginning of familiarizing with the image of the Self. I had questions and the questions kept spiraling. I went through books after books, listened to talks, speeches from many influencers, spiritual leaders and did a lot of self-reflection eventually. As my analytical self was in action, I started observing a lot of coincidences in the past. Things like, if I had not been in a certain place, at a certain time, I may not have met a certain person, or an opportunity and certain things may have manifested differently. What determined these coincidences? Are they just random? This curiosity over coincidences led me to the search for the Doer. The self-reflection started with taking different segments of my life to see who the actual doer was. Where did it all start. It was difficult to find anything over mundane things. So, I decided to go with a more impactful memory from the past. To me, a major path determining factor of my life was the strong desire to live free, like the women in the West did, as per the me in my early teens. The women of the west seemed strong, independent, working, free. I liked that. And I wanted it for me. This desire probably led me to achieving the exact same life, in a span of 10-15 years, after a lot of ups and downs. It all almost manifested with coincidences. It did happen though - I feel free. Just the way I imagined I would. And this feeling is something I treasure deeply. The question to me now was, that how did this desire even come to me at the first place? What made me desire this? So, I dug a bit more. I analyzed my past. My memories of past. A strong influence were probably women I watched on television or read about or met, who lived in the west and spoke about the life there and how they carried themselves. I often thought to myself - that must be nice. To be independent, dress the way you want, do what you want, take decisions for yourself. Growing up, I enjoyed a lot of freedom myself, but this felt different. The kind of freedom these women enjoyed. I couldn't put my finger on what it was that seemed different. So ultimately, it was the environment I was born in, that brought in that desire in the first place. But where I was born was not in my hands. It was my destiny. As I started connecting the dots, one thing led to the other and I could clearly see the well-orchestrated plan that was made for me, so I could be where I am today. I didn't start it, I am not going to end it. I am just leading it – this path that a higher energy has designed for me. We call them coincidences because to our ego Self, it's not something we planned for ourselves, but they aren't coincidences to the One that has laid a path for you to take. You can call the One - God, higher power, cosmic energy, a mathematical equation, randomness, a law…. a force that's operating beyond us. An awareness we are unaware of fully.

The desires, thoughts, dreams are in the Doer for you. Your job is not to find your purpose in life but to find what is the purpose for you in the cosmic force that brought you here. And whatever step I am taking - knowingly, unknowingly is always the right path. There is only one path. The path laid down by the cosmic force that brought you to this world. The path maybe bumpy occasionally, the path maybe breezy at other times. But it is your path taking you where you need to be, realizing and erasing what you have learnt and what you haven't learnt, on the way.

It's a deepening experience. Life only deepens as you move forward till you find the source that brought you to existence. Often a lifetime isn't enough. Experiences help you deepen, realizations help you deepen in someone else's life. It eventually becomes a collective process. You see the depth in everything around you.

Why does it Hurt?

An impactful experience like getting hurt, comes with a deep message that goes unnoticed in the wake of sorrow it accompanies. And you often hear such heartbreaks amongst the younger generation who are in the prime of their youth. Whose eyes are filled with dreams that the world around shows them. Every aspect of the ego is well defined in their mind – recognition, attention, love, pride, pleasure, and they seek for it in anything that's outside of them. Many inevitably have a great fall and get hurt. They often come out of it with a question of whether they are self-worthy or even deserve love. Many question their physical attributes. For those who are meant to learn early, this becomes a turning point for introspection. It's a transformative phase, their perspective towards the external environment changes. Pain has the power to transform if one pays attention. Hurting and healing are repetitive learning processes in life. At times, it's you are hurting someone and the other times it's you are getting hurt. As we progress in life, we ought to do things that could be hurtful to someone. We don't really realize the impact of our doing in their life at that very moment. But that hurtful experience teaches the other person an important lesson, if it is time for their progress. They learn and progress. Because often when it hurts, you start paying attention. Now as you move forward in life, you one day reach the point, where the other person was. You get hurt and you progress. You particularly progress with two important lessons now. Every action has a purpose and an equal opposite reaction that also has a purpose. Here the purpose of action was the progress of the other and the purpose of the reaction is your progress. Second, you learn empathy and forgiveness. You understand the hurt you caused someone in the past. You feel for them. You also learn to forgive the one that's hurting you now. Hence it is important for a reaction to follow the actions you take. There is a better understanding of the grand scheme of plans. How everything is a give and take. You give hurt, you get hurt. You give love, you get love. You give kindness, you get kindness. It's the formula of learning that the cosmic force has designed. So, you understand both sides of the coin. You get the complete picture. Simply because, you are never only the hero. You are both the hero and the villain. But both the hero and villain create what is called life. You are never only the one. No one is just only the one. Having this understanding later in life, also gives you the wisdom of not letting someone hurt you. People and circumstances can only hurt you when you let them. When you give out an action, they can react to. They often hurt you by taking away what our ego desires the most. Keeping your ego in check and at bare minimum leaves nothing for the second person to work with. When you aren't expecting anything from another person, there is really nothing the other person can take away from you. But how do you truly reach a point where you are not expecting anything from someone? How does one reach a point where they are already fulfilled from within, when most today are looking for comfort, company and compassion? They are either looking for recognition or support. A simple answer is by paying attention and engaging with yourself. Seeking answers from the Self. It may take some practice but if one follows it diligently, its starts building confidence within themselves to know what's right for them, and they stop looking for answers outside of them. One start rejoicing their own company. You are just here to coexist and fulfil the purpose that the Doer has for you in whatever shape and form and when your focus becomes that, everything happening around starts making more sense.

A lot of times people come into your life and then leave. It's hard to understand the purpose of their arrival, and later their departure. Until years later, you see the impact of the person's presence and absence in your life and how in some way it's led to where you are today. There are countless people in my life, who have made a similar impact. It doesn't seem less than a wonder how everything in the universe conspired to bring them into my life to create a lifelong impact. My closest friend came into my life when I was nine years old. Our friendship continued for years and years later, even though we didn't live in the same town anymore. Those were the days of no cellphones and emails. We wrote handwritten letters to each other every month. She saw me through my biggest ups and downs. She was a sister / friend to me from the very beginning. Least did I know, she will be the instrument used by the Doer against all odds, in meeting the person I am sharing the rest of my life with today. Especially, given the situation I was in - divorced, in a foreign land away from my home country and finding it hard to connect with anyone authentically, so to share rest of the life with again. Chances of me meeting someone across the oceans and being able to go past the barriers of distance, inhibitions and misunderstandings was no less than a plan made by some force that's higher than me. And the fact that my friend from my childhood would be the reason for this impact, was gratifying and no less astonishing. It was not just the result that seemed miraculous but every detail of event that happened. There was a clear sign of destiny. So, anytime a person walks into your life, understand the purpose they are here for. Are they merely here for what seems obvious or is there a deeper purpose lying underneath? This will particularly help you in the scenarios when they are no longer with you, and you feel lost, hurt and confused. They sometimes come bearing a message or the other times they come to learn something from you by engaging in experiences. Having this disclaimer back of your mind helps you stay detached.

The moment you realize the pre orchestration, you feel a sense of ease and you develop a mindset of sitting back, relax and watch life as an exciting movie playing ahead of you with some brilliant script writing. And then to know the millions and billions of lives that exists, that's conscious, gets to have a story of their own… Brilliance of the Doer!

Blame game

I find blame game the biggest divide of humanity. It's coming from the belief of the right and wrong path. How can there be a right and wrong when every path is leading you to the Ultimate. Every path is different and unique but are they right and wrong? People bless you to always take the right path. Does that blessing hold any substance in reality? It's the very "rights" and "wrongs" that takes you forward in your path. So then, does a choice here make any sense? Does it leave any room for introspection? The very universe we know is moving towards its end. Does that mean the universe is on the wrong path? To us death is the not something most of us look forward to. Most dread it. Yet, we all are destined to leave this human body someday. Does that mean we are on the wrong path, ultimately achieving what we dread the most? The moment you divide the path as right and wrong, you bring in the ego. The ego that deludes you, masking the real cosmic force, the Doer. You start believing, it's everyone's ego that's the Doer. The very contradiction here is that ego on one hand deludes itself to be the Doer but at the same time doesn't think it's perfect. Hence the divide of right and wrong arises. The ego somewhere knows its flawed. It doesn't hold a substantial existence.

Ego is here to connect you with the Ultimate. The ego is like a transcriber, transcribing the language of the Doer. But, in doing so, sometimes it's starts mistaking or deluding itself to be the Doer. And imperfectly in thinking so, it starts seeing separation.

Separation brings divide of right and wrong. This creates the room for blame, entangling the path furthermore. It's nothing but a huge challenge to unwind what's been created by the ego but nothing here is without a purpose. This entangling also comes with its purpose and time will tell why the chaos was created in our minds. For now, understanding it's a chaos is good enough for the progress.

Love, loss and life

The biggest teachers of truth.

Sometimes you love someone deeply. And you don't get the same in return. It gives you a deep sense of loss. You wonder why you can't stop obsessing or loving someone who doesn't feel the same. Or why is the other person incapable of reciprocation. It's a multilayered process of learning. First is the layer of your ego that's telling you, you are doing something inadequate, and so you are not receiving what you think you deserve. This gives you the most pain and agony. So, you start doing things that your ego is suggesting. Chances are that your desires will remain unfulfilled long term. Now that things are not going your way, and you have exhausted all the suggestions of your ego, you start recognizing the powerlessness of ego. This realization opens the layer of a Self, that's beyond the ego. You decide to turn towards your inner self which isn't always as loud as your ego. Its more subtle but always present. You start the inner search of why it is not working. There is someone within you, that seems to know the answer. You come face to face. You start understanding the process a little more now. Your strong desire is still very fresh, but you start engaging with yourself. And then comes the final layer of learning. It's time for your actual destiny. After your deep understanding of your Self beyond the ego, when the judgement comes- whether your desire will be fulfilled or not, you are now equipped to withstand the result. It prepares you for the result. Simply because now, you are looking at things very differently. You don't have the eye of the ego. You are seeing through the eye of the Self. Until the vision doesn't change from the ego to the Self, experiences keep repeating themselves in some form or the other till you get polished and shine like a diamond. The result may or may not be your desire getting fulfilled but you sure will understand the purpose of why the desire took its birth in you in the first place and what were you to accomplish from it. So instead of feeling a sense of loss, you see what you have gained from the experience.

This translates to loss of loved ones, loss of success, loss of any kind of desires, a job you once wanted .... Anything. Life teaches you through your unfulfilled desires because that's the most efficient way to get your attention. It's usually when a strong desire you had, that goes unfulfilled, no matter how bad you wanted it or how hard you try, you see the powerlessness of your ego self, that thinks it can do what it wants without connecting to its authentic power. Until then no matter how much you hear or learn about something that's beyond your ego, you really can't seem to place anything in control other than your ego. And the moment we are in the delusion of ego being the Doer, nothing but uncertainty and restlessness awaits us. It's like asking a wild horse to take you home. Unfulfilled desires are painful, but they are also the biggest resource to dive deep within. Dive deep within to see, why is it not working. And eventually what is it that's not working ....

Many might wonder, then what about those who die with their desires unfulfilled. We are not here to fulfill our desires. We are here to serve our purpose. The cosmic force that brings you to this world makes sure the purpose is fulfilled before you transcend into a different form, with a newer, higher purpose and the progress continues ...

Many associate purposes with materialistic riches. A lot of times a beggar is looked upon purposeless, worthless and meaningless. What possibly could be a purpose of a beggar in this world. Only here to suffer. Dying a death of pain and misery. A purpose doesn't come in ways and forms defined by us as higher and lower. A purpose is a purpose. A homeless person, taking care of a dog might be serving the purpose of showing compassion and love and learning the same from another species, in a way that it connects him to a deeper sense of Self. Such a man has achieved his purpose as opposed to someone who has all wealth in the world but is lost in the cycle of ego and power. To this rich man, having wealth and not knowing how to use it in a way that can give him true contentment, is the learning opportunity. To the beggar, not having wealth but to lead a meaningful life is the learning opportunity. Whatever it is, the force that brings you to life, makes sure your purpose here is done for the time you are here, in this form and energy. It's futile to think one comes with a purpose and the other doesn't.

Every wave of supreme comes to the shore, that's your ego, brings a new lesson and once its purpose is done, it goes back into the ocean of consciousness, again to come back to a new ego, as a new wave, with a new purpose.

The nature around us is a metaphor to the many truths of life. The changing seasons are reflecting that nothing is permanent. Everything is changing. But every change here has a purpose and strikes a balance in the law of nature. No season is purposeless in the cycle of life. Everything around is also cyclic in nature. It changes from one form to the other. Soul, the spiritual energy also transcends from one form to other, bringing changes and a new purpose with it, as it travels.

It is also important to honor the journey of the other. Today might be your day of letting go. Letting go of judgements, anger, anxiety. A sense of control. Often when one reaches this point, we can easily get distracted by ignorance of others. This gives birth to a tendency of seeing wrong in everybody just because they don't perceive things the way you do. I still struggle with this even today and so I try to find ways to invoke compassion and not judgement. It's important to remind yourself of what you are letting go and that honoring another person's journey is equally as important as yours. Everybody is learning and ultimately wanting to let go and figure it out deep down. Everyone is on the path of achieving their milestone. Some know it as much as you do, some may know more than you do and yet there may be many who are just not there yet. It's okay. You show your kindness and love and everything you wish you would have had when you didn't know, what you know now.

Accepting the role of a student and teacher helps you let go of the judgment. Once you realize you are here to learn and teach, you start seeing purpose in everything. With some you learn, and with some others, you become the source of inspiration.

Suffering

Suffering is one of the most potent drugs. It has the power to jump you over multiple levels when you are going up the ladder of life, trying to reach the ultimate truth. Often when I saw immense suffering in the past, it brought me grief. Suffering not just in me but others as well. We all feel the pain. Today, I look at suffering differently. Suffering is an indicator that someone's life is going to change. The reason being that suffering reduces you down to your truest naked self. It's a chance to restart, revision your life; a clean slate to rewrite your story with all the learnings you had on your way so far. They are here to bring in a big change in your perspective about life. Now this change may or may not be visible in the physical realm but it's a change apparent to the heart of the one going through it. It would be a very personal experience to them. Suffering remains a suffering till one is choosing to suffer. It is the toughest path to endeavor but the most rewarding one as well. One only suffers till their perspective remains the same. The moment the vision changes, suffering slowly fades away. To understand this shift, one needs to go through the difficult phase of breaking the bubble they are molded in by their ego. One suffers as the bubble breaks, but soon you blossom out free and eventually leaving the body much closer to the higher power.

There was a time when I thought I lost it all - the love, the shelter of my parents and other close extended family members, the familiarity of my own country I was born in and more painfully so, the dream I had for my future. Most importantly, until then, my ego thought it had it all or that I could do something in the realm of ego, if I did what's right to fix things for me but all it did was continue the suffering. Today when I look back, that was the most inspiring and uplifting phase of my life. With all the pain and suffering came so much perspective of life that I couldn't look at anything less than a miracle anymore. It brought me closest to the Doer. It grounded me and anchored me strongly to my soul. I have never looked at worries and suffering the same way again. They do come and go because that's life. But they don't leave the same impact. You are different now and you treat them differently. Your vision changes, the world around you changes. Suffering takes away the layer of unreal, you were encapsulated in. Now you are naked. For a moment you feel powerless. And then one rises with the real authentic power we are all born with. Power that shows you what matters and what really doesn't in this life and if it the right time for you, you adapt to this power and start experiencing a change of aura within you. That is the potential change a suffering can bring in one's life.

The mantra

When it's time, it will come.

I couldn't swear on anything more than this mantra. This was not an overnight realization. It came in bits and pieces of small and big experiences. But on observing, it appeared to be consistent in almost anything. Be it my first car, first job, my life partner, baby or even writing this book. The thought comes way ahead but the actual manifestation happens when you are ready for it. The gap between the thoughts and manifestations is the biggest struggle for many. The wait, the anxiety, the result. Will I get it, or not get it? Am I doing enough to get it? If it's something you are meant to receive, you are probably getting prepared for it, even without your knowing. You may only realize about all the preparation that went into getting you ready, once after you receive it. It makes more sense at that time as to why there is a right time for everything and how unprepared you were when a desire just sprouted within your heart. Preparation helps you understand the path and purpose of the desire, in your life. If anytime you desire something but end up not getting them fulfilled, then a lack of understanding of the purpose can misguide you. Do not be mistaken on the purpose of the desire. Something was hiding behind the mask of that desire that was ahead of you. You probably didn't get the obvious desire, but you would have achieved the actual purpose behind that desire that sprouted in you.

The greatest challenge is to live through these gaps of realization. To be patient and see things with the correct vision. One who achieves it, finds peace. One who is learning or a beginner, feels lost and distressed often. But everyone gets there. Today or tomorrow. Everyone does. No one is left behind in achieving this vision to see the path and purpose of desires and the timelines in which they manifest. Awakenings changes our vision in how we perceive desires. The mantra to follow between the sprouting of the desire and the manifestation of its purpose is to give it time. Time is everything here. Until then observe with a keen mind, what are the changes coming into being. How is the path getting created. Be an observer. The preparation that needs to go in is already in place. You are to experience it in awareness, so to fulfill the purpose behind the desire.

Love and freedom

Love and freedom are complimentary. If you love, you are free. If you are free, you love. The question is what kind of love brings freedom and what kind of freedom invokes love. You don't need anything to love, you don't need anything to feel free. Rather you feel free and loved when you are not bound by anything. This very fact tells you what kind of love is more authentic and unwavering. The one that gives you sense of attachment and bondage is not necessarily the love that brings peace. It's a different kind of love in a lower form. Certainly not invalid. Nothing here is. Everything is here to teach you the true definition of the higher entity it represents. Romantic love is very often mistaken as love. It is love but not the love in its highest form because it often comes with bondage. It's a love that shows you a glimpse of the love or emotion that is very universal and we all feel it, know it without anyone teaching it to you. Freedom is also a form of higher truth. You feel free when you are detached. Now what does that really mean? To be detached. How can a mother be detached from her child? Is that even a valid emotion? True detachment comes when you no longer feel a control over someone's path or need to control someone's path. Even your own child and his or her own destiny. It's important to honor their purpose and their path. Whatever that maybe. It's the toughest thing to let go. Especially, because it's difficult to detach your children from you. It's difficult to see them as a creation of the universe and not your own creation. It's difficult to see them suffer. And hence we suffer the attachment and expectation, unable to free yourself or the child. We want the best for them, but we don't realize often the higher purpose they are here for. Which they will lead irrespective of your control. All that the sense of control does is, either take away the love or take away the freedom or both, that you deserve.

Anything we try hard to hold on to is not permanent because you are having to try hard to hold on to it. The moment you let go of something you were trying hard to hold on to, beneath the surface floats freedom. Freedom that feels like peace. Peace that will feel like love. It's what you get once you filter out all that you thought was permanent. All that your ego thought is the source of freedom, peace and love. And once the force of cosmos, forces you to let go through different failures and success, you learn what's beneath and what it feels like. It's the game of masking and unmasking.

How to be?

The question arises then as to how is one to lead the path without being in control. A numbness often seeps in when you first realize the lack of your control, of your ego self. The truth is though that life moves on and you move on with it too but with a new perspective and a new vision. At first not having control may seem limiting but as you progress one realizes how liberating it is, instead. The surroundings remain the same, but you are looking at things differently now. That is the purpose of realization. It doesn't change what already exists but what changes is your perspective on looking at things. For instance, if everything is destined are we to then help others? Are we to give advice? What changes now is your intention behind the advice. You give advice with the understanding that it may or may not have a purpose in the life its going out to or that maybe the timing is not right. You give it with an intention that, if it's meant to be, it's going to work, if not then perhaps there is a different path laid out for the other person in the Doer. And you move forward unaffected, detached and in peace.

How about worries, bad days and the days you feel like the energy isn't quite up there? The more you are closer to realizing the purpose aspect of your living, centering yourself becomes much easier. Worries and distress don't fade away. Nothing fades away. The world runs as it is. Just that they don't affect you the same way anymore. The frequency and intensity changes drastically. It lessens tremendously. The deeper you go within yourself, the more you realize the Doer and the more your ego feels the powerlessness and less is the chatter in your head of the superficial self. There is a steady current of calmness. Once your awareness starts shifting, you experience a withdrawal from your sensory impulses. The need to feed your ego declines. Acceptance develops. You no longer thrive on external surroundings for answers. Your inner self starts communicating with you much louder than the external voices. A discipline sets in your life.

Discipline

I find the cosmos to be a very method based, law-based entity. Trying to apply the same principles of cosmos in my day-to-day life brought in some great revelations. Consistency seems to be the underlying current of stillness. When things follow a rhythm and pattern, stillness is more easily achievable.

Has repetition, consistency, method, discipline changed the trajectory of my life? Have I observed such patterns in my life? Short answer is, yes. I have a routine now. Following it has become a way of life. I give it a lot of credit for the peace and settlement I have in my life. But, until I didn't self-reflect on it, I did not realize how much impact it had on getting me a clear vision that often got muggy in the clutter of mind before. My first two hours of the day as soon as I wake up, has become my most important two hours of the day. All the tools I have been given when I was born are placed in front of me - intentions, desires, thoughts, ego, visions and above all self-reflections on the purpose. What I consume and reflect upon during that time generally sets the pattern for the day. Silence becomes the biggest teacher. It also gives me great opportunity to put my ego in check. If I go days without following this method, I find myself under the attack of ego. And the divide of good and bad seeps in. The morning routine helps me look at the same problems and worries quite differently. I always wondered what universal love would feel like. What does it mean to see God in everything? The moment you are still and connected in a self-reflective mode, you see yourself in others. In other things. How you could be them in their circumstances. You start relating to the experiences of others as if they are your own. We all know these things but to really realize and feel it from heart doesn't come easy. But when it does, a unique sense of oneness comes in. All our goals seem to be unified. We all are looking for the same thing from different resources. Hoping to someday transform my entire day into the first two hours of my day. It will be a huge milestone for me and my journey to the Self. I find the self-reflection a prayer to the higher power, the connect to the higher power. The connection that often gets lost in the chatter of experiences we have daily. To take a moment and to be still, is like a shot of espresso. It awakens you almost instantly as you practice it more and more in your life. What the Doer teaches here is the essence of discipline in things. As you progress in spirituality, discipline becomes a way of being. The universe and its bodies follow the discipline of birth, death and survival. The bodily functions that are not in the control of the ego follows discipline. Your heart, kidneys, lungs, liver all follow their discipline in bodily functions and accommodate the changes that the body experiences. Everything is in auto mode. What the mind needs is the same auto mode to carryout love and freedom that it is supposed to carry out and accommodate the changes that life throws at it as to maintain the balance, without wavering from the core values of the Self. And that's exactly what life achieves eventually but until we aren't aware, we are oblivious to these changes of accommodation and balance. You must start somewhere. It's also important not to get disheartened when you can't seem to figure out meditation and stillness. The very fact that you have a desire to experience it means it's coming along for you. The timeline maybe different for different people but everyone is getting there.

The very fact that this thought has bubbled in your heart means it's something you can anticipate for the future. That the cosmic force is telling you that a change is coming. You need to keep your mind and heart open.

The Ego 'I'

It's a fact to grasp that everything here is valid - good, bad as we humans call it. And nothing is in the control of the ego. But, to understand this, it's very important to understand what the ego is. Anything that gives you a sense of divide is the ego. The moment you feel you are different from the other, ego is taking its form. So, it's also important to understand what exactly is different and what isn't. To our physical senses, there are 100s of differences between two things we see around us. But, if you look from a deeper perspective, when your mind is centered, you will observe what makes everything one. The journey from the vision of difference to the vision of oneness is the journey of life. However, how we feel or see now is ok. It's your journey and with each experience, with each revelation, comes your progress.

When you aren't bound by anything anymore, the ego 'I' fades away. It cannot exist without attaching itself to something. I am wise, I am beautiful, I am angry, I am victimized, I am proud, I am sad, I am happy.... Anything that tells you, you are something that's not permanent, is your ego self. Anything that shows you, something that is permanent, and nothing can take it away from you, is your higher Self. The question one needs to ask themselves is what that's permanent in their life and what brought it in to their lives. This could be a turning point for those who are lost in the dilemma of what's real and what is not real. One can go to the greatest mystics in the world for answers and clarity but until and unless they don't self-realize these truths about their own lives, one feels lost and often misguided. So, when the timing is right, the right guidance and some self-realization can unmask the veil the ego 'I' casts on the higher Self, the Doer. The ego is highly alluring and something we are most familiar with. It is very much a part of you. The important thing here is to know what the ego is here for. Often ego is looked upon as the bad guy. If used and tamed properly, ego can be the biggest instrument to show you the depth of who you truly are. Realization is a relative process. It is the journey from the obvious superficial self and to the Doer within. By isolating ego, we find the door that opens to the Doer. If it wasn't for the ego, that often gives you an unsettling life, would we ever find the necessity to seek the Doer or the real Self? It's when we cannot figure it out with what we have externally that we turn inwards. To me, the worth of what's internal comes from a comparison of what's lacking outside - often a feeling of hollow that makes you turn inwards and eventually you start feeling full again. Complete. And so it's a relative process for me. The point is that nothing is invalid in this journey of life .Every single thing that exists, be it the ego, misery, happiness, triumph is all here to take you forward or in another sense to take you back to your origin .The Doer in you sets the curriculum for the learning. And we like it or not but the very villain that is the ego, is your biggest guiding force to your true higher Self.

There is often a thin line between the ego and self-respect. How to tell the difference? In simple terms ego attaches and self-respect detaches. If you take a scenario where someone is hurting you, and you decide to move away, detach yourself from your ego and someone else's ego. It is keeping your self respect. You accomplish the job to safeguard your 'Self'. A scenario where someone is necessarily not doing things your way and you decide to act against it, more often involves the ego because you are attached to your opinion and when someone is not following your way, it disappoints you and out of frustration and anger you decide to punish the other in some way or the other. Self-respect is enabling yourself to find the center no matter what the external circumstances are. Self-respect is honoring the voice, the whisper that's within you that's always showing what you want deep down within. To hear and honor it is self-respect. Ego on the other hand is safeguarding something that's not permanent. Its safeguarding your pride, your anger, your stubbornness, your grief, your pleasure. What it is not safeguarding is your center. So then how does one practice self-respect over ego? Humility is one way. Keeping your humility helps you anchor yourself to your center. Humility is a giving process. Letting go of pride and achievements. It's in portraying yourself to be a learner. Idea is to project the learner in you always but also have the understanding within that you may sometimes be the teacher. Being a learner, you can admit but being a teacher is something that should be acknowledged by others. One shouldn't be seeking validation for being a teacher. No one needs a validation to be a learner, but teacher seeks validation. So don't seek what needs validation. Because validation attaches and the moment attachment comes, ego sets in, and you move away from the center. Validation is also a form of divide. You are better than someone. What can such a thought bring to you other than eventual jealousy, envy and competition?

Self-Inquiry

In microbiology, a cultural medium is a suitable environment for a microorganism to grow. Self-Realization also grows in suitable medium. It often starts with outer discipline, followed by inner discipline. Outer discipline means setting a schedule for yourself daily and being consistent with whatever it is that you plan. Persistence and consistency are the most important factors here. This also involves keeping your external environment organized. Keeping your room organized, your work, your eating habits, your workouts, your social habits, your leisure time and then the time with your Self. Its taming your five senses to be disciplined. For beginners, time with your Self could be meditation, taking some time alone with your thoughts or just practicing silence. Something that you practice alone. And then comes inner discipline. Practicing silence fine-tunes the voice of the Doer. Silence not just when you are sitting alone but also when you have the at most urge to speak your opinion or defend yourself or offend someone. Practicing silence in such scenarios is a huge challenge. But the more you follow it, the more centered you become. One shall notice, as you set yourself out in this journey, you'll attract more and more people who come as a confirmation to what your next path should be. Now that you are more organized you can see the message of the Doer clearly, that they are bringing into your life. A warning though -not everyone is bringing the message in an envelope of joy. Some may come as challenges. But you are equipping yourself to go beyond the outer hard shell and get to the inner core of where the real message lies. Inner discipline also involves practicing humility and recognizing the ego. Just paying attention every time your ego surfaces and trying not to act upon it. Eventually, you will see your mind more organized. You sorrow and happiness are more organized. Now you have created a suitable environment for further growth. A suitable cultural medium. To this when you add a pinch of Self-Inquiry, magic happens. Self-Inquiry becomes a turning point here. Otherwise, you are just a person with good habits in human terms. What makes the difference is the quest or search for the Doer within you. Many ask the question 'why' in the state of misery or sorrow but to ask the 'why' in a state of peace is what's the difference. When you see yourself searching and looking for an answer with a centered mind, you have hit a milestone. This is an excellent time to look back and connect the dots as to how every big, small detail of events that happened in your life brought you to this point, where you are today. You say thank you to those experiences, good or bad and take up the journey of Self-Inquiry. Sometimes it takes more than a lifetime to reach this point. And for some others it comes as a flash of lightening. We all are progressing towards it.

Anytime you see someone being ignorant, drunk in ego don't resent them or despise them. Believe in their journey, believe in their progress and believe that however they are being right now has a higher purpose. If there are n number of humans on this earth, then there are n number of paths to self-realization. There might be many parallels amongst these paths and lot many times differences too.

The Illusion

When you advance on the path of Self-realization, you realize that to experience life is like watching a movie but with one major difference. One experiences different emotions watching a movie. Sometimes joy, sometimes excitement, sometimes pain, thrill, grief and so on. You may also experience boredom, offense and anger with some others. All kinds of emotions. But none of these emotions are ever personal to you, no matter how much you relate to them. If the movie is impactful enough, you may experience its impact for days after you have watched the movie. Yet at the back of the mind, you know it's only a movie. So, you can separate the real from the unreal. You are aware of the illusion that the movie and the movie creators have created. You understand the purpose as well. So, you feel all those emotions, but you don't take them personally and with time you are able to let go. A person advancing in Self-Realization is made to understand this reality of life by the Doer through realizations of the purpose. So now the person experiences life with all its emotions but back of their mind, the person is aware of the higher purpose that lies underneath the sheath of illusion that appears in front of us.

    This understanding is important because it keeps compassion and empathy alive towards those who haven't advanced on this path. For them, the pain, suffering, joys and desires are the very reality of life, and it is very rightly so for where they are. They feel the burden of having to make things happen on their shoulders. They feel the need to control their lives. The Self-realized understands this because they have been there. They once passed such a phase. With such realizations of the realized and the unrealized, the Doer balances the role of teacher and student.

The illusion is the very life. But why do we call it illusion when everything appears so real? It appears real because it is apparent, and it is the language we understand. It is created to teach us a higher truth. But the concept of illusion can confuse us. Lot of people mistake illusion for irrelevance when they first familiarize with the concept. Just because something is an illusion doesn't mean it's irrelevant. Your pain, suffering or even joy and success maybe an illusion but it is created to teach you something deeper and more important. So, they are certainly not irrelevant and nothing to feel guilty about. If you feel sad and lost today, it is relevant. Because only when you are lost, you can find yourself again. So, to say no one should feel any pain or joy doesn't hold any ground. The important thing is to look for the purpose behind this illusion. Why are you really feeling the pain, why are you joyous, why is something not lasting? Why are you feeling stuck? Why do you feel the anger? Why do you feel the need to control? Why do you fear? This introspection exercise is a great tool to help you find the source as you practice it more. But foremost one must recognize it is an illusion to even began the journey of introspection. To seek what is behind the illusion and who is creating it and why.

Choice

What is a choice? Why is it important? Choice is an important concept to understand when we discuss the Doer. First, we need to ask ourselves, why is choice important to us? Why is it important for me to know if I have a choice? What is the benefit of having a choice? There might be multiple answers coming to the mind right now. Like, I need to know if I have a choice so I can take the right decisions in life, I can bring joy, happiness and prosperity to my life, I can live upto my complete potential, I can motivate others to do make the right choice. In short, we all want to do the right things for us and our loved ones with the choices we make. However, when you speak of a right choice, you are inevitably giving birth to a wrong choice as well. Now this creates a divide. Divide brings in the ego that masks the reality of the rights and wrong. It's the rights and wrongs in your life that has brought you where you are. On one hand where the rights may have encouraged you to move forward, it's the wrongs that taught you the lessons you will need as you move forward. So, you are benefitting from both, then how is one right and the other wrong? If we really had a choice, every human on Earth would do only what's right for them. And the world would be a very different place today. The very fact that we are a result of the rights and wrongs tells you, you need both to progress in this strange engineering called life that the Doer has designed. The choice doesn't exist to do the right or wrong. The choice that exists is the one to understand or not why a choice was made for you. What was the purpose behind the choice.

Rights and wrongs are nothing but the words and pauses of a musical note. A song is incomplete without either. We may have approvals and disapprovals from others regarding the choices we make. What is food for one may be the death for the other. What is right for one, may be wrong for the other. Good and bad, right and wrong are relative terms. They are not universal. Hence, even souls like Buddha, Christ and so many suffered in the hands of those to whom these souls were making the wrong choices, when all they did was follow the right path according to them and majority of others even today. The major difference here is the perception of these great souls who never focused on the suffering. They never focused on the words and pauses. They rather focused on the great music that the combination of the two was creating for the world to hear. So, understand what a choice is and where exactly it operates. Once such a clarity comes your way a pressure is lifted off your shoulder. You become much more accepting of things that are happening around you but at the same time you understand the learning behind what is happening and why it is happening. The moment you think it is your choice, you are attaching yourself to the result of your choices. If I do this, I should get this. Or things should happen this way. If things were so simple and straight forward, we wouldn't be lost and in despair. The fact that we are in this illusion causes the suffering. So, changing the focus from if I have a choice to why was a choice made for me helps you prepare for the path that's laid down for you. As you move forward, you start understanding the process more and more. Its liberating. Marching forward with this awareness helps you focus on the purpose behind everything rather than the suffering.

Purpose

How does one define purpose? Purpose is the reason of your being. You are here for the purpose; you fulfill while you take a life form in the universe. This is true in a scientific sense and a spiritual sense. Does that mean we all come here with 'a' purpose and once that's achieved, we are left with no reason of being? Purpose is an ongoing process and not one single thing to achieve in life. It's in the evolution of your consciousness. Every step you are taking is a step towards this evolution knowingly or unknowingly. Our job is to cut down the outer clutter and tune inwards to see what the purpose in the very moment is. Why are you here? what is it that you really want deep down? Practice by observing what materialistic things do you wish to achieve and then try eliminating them one by one until you reach an unmaterialistic purpose underlying the materialistic desire. For instance, if you think your purpose today, where you are at this point in life, in the present, is to have financial stability. You dig a bit more by asking why do need financial stability. As an example, say your answer is, so you can get the comforts of life for you and your family. Next is to ask yourself what the comforts would bring into your life. If the answer is stability, or joy or happiness, which mostly is, then ask yourself what happiness would bring into your life. Why do you want to be happy? If the answer lies somewhere as-who doesn't wish to be happy, then understand why you do like being happy. What does it mean to be happy? Are you able to express it? Fully see it.

We come from a source that's ultimate, and we are evolving back into the ultimate. The true nature of the Ultimate is fullness. Contentment. Nothing to take, only to give and create.

Happiness is in contentment. Hence, we all seek it deep down within, in whichever shape and form it comes. But where we fail is in holding on to it. When you are content, you are happy. Our purpose in life is to reach this contentment and be able to hold on to it. The latter is a much higher purpose, but our immediate goal is to find the contentment. What makes you content? And once you achieve it, the immediate next question should be, how can I make it last? Understanding contentment is understanding your purpose. Once you understand contentment, you give yourself a promise to never dishonor it. You strive for the contentment without fearing guilt or suspicion of suffering. Only a content purpose can give the surrounding what it lacks. They don't look at the suffering, therefore. Rather they look at it as a price you pay to achieve your purpose. Just like one is willing to spend thousands of dollars on an expensive car they desire, one is willing to go through the suffering as soon as they realize where their contentment lies. Our job is to figure out where the contentment lies and then honor the path that leads you to it.

Money

It is important to understand the relation we have with money today. Simply because of the power we have given it and the control it has over us today. My relationship with money has been varying. Growing up, we had enough but not surplus to splurge. And then came a point when I was starting from scratch, building my life on my own terms. Worked two jobs and went to a grad school, all at the same time. Making just enough to afford the rent and some comforts. Finally, I was on my own feet, with a white-collar job that gives me enough to splurge if I choose to. All this time, if money has taught me anything, it is that the more you keep it flowing, the least it sticks to you and the freer you are. The more you hold on to it, the more it gains power over you. This is the hardest thing to understand because no one wants the kind of suffering that involves financial scarcity. But the problem is we don't know when money is enough. The more you have it, the scarcer you feel. I have often noticed when I place my true values over money, I always have more money than what I anticipated in my bank account. The more I worry about money, the poorer my bank account seems to be. It's very interesting and there is a constant voice inside me that says don't let it stick to you. It is also a great learning lesson as to why it is important to let go and what is important to let go. What holds you back, takes you away from your center. Once you realize what you aim for in life, your goal is to create a space to manifest it. If the space is not created, one suffers. For instance, if I strive for contentment but worry about not having enough money, I am taking away the space to feel contentment. So, what is the solution? Do we keep on focusing on money, to feel the contentment one day? Has that ever worked for anyone? The question isn't what you have. The question should be what are you doing with what you have? That answers the question of why you have lack of contentment. Ultimately, what is it that money is bringing into your life. To many money brings power. Wouldn't it be better if you already have power and then have the money and not the other way around? But then how do you get that sort of power that money cannot buy? It comes from within you. It comes from the wisdom of letting go of anything you wish for, that money must buy for you and then seek for contentment. And once you find contentment in this manner, you gain power over money. It is however also important to understand what kind of energy money brings around you or the people around you. On one hand, when it is important to not let the money have the power over you, it is also important to not let go of the value money can bring into the lives of those who need it or the causes you wish to support. You are the only one who can give the right value and power to money that you have earned. So, you do hold the responsibility of channeling it to the right path. Just like suffering, money is also here to be a great teacher. So, understanding its purpose is freeing yourself.

A Piece of Me

Born in Cochin, India, to my parents, I was raised with love, care and support. Life wasn't always a bed of roses but there were enough comforts. My father was in the military and mother was a teacher. They both were dedicated professionals and homemakers at the same time. When I look back at my childhood, the greatest gift my parents have given me is compassion. They taught my brother and I to be compassionate. I always wonder how they achieved this. What did they say or do that made us value compassion? Or is it something innate you get genetically. How did they teach us to be nice?

Growing up, I was ambitious and a dreamer. I was greatly influenced by the self-made souls and especially women of the west and wanted to live like them-free. I wanted the freedom to be whom I wanted to be and live the way I wanted to live. Although I came from a very liberal and supportive family, we did have some societal pressures on how a girl is supposed to be especially when she reaches her adolescence. It would be fair enough to say, starting from late teens began the most testing phase of my life which went about for another decade or so. It started getting harder to work with emotions, expectations and self-worth, all at the same time. It was always about picking one over the others. It affected my academics at some very crucial points. I couldn't focus and deliver academically the same way I use to. I had the greatest fall in my twelfth Grade when I barely made it. I went from being the topper of the class to almost the bottom list. Shame and despair took over. I felt very disappointed and found it hard to face those who believed in me, especially my parents and my Uncle I looked up to and was very close to me. When you let down those who encourage you the most, its most heart breaking. I survived by some Grace, but then I hit the rock bottom, and I gave myself a promise-never again! There was a determination in me that I won't let any thought distract me from my academics. Least did I know there were greater lessons waiting for me. But this was my first episode of introspection with the Self, analyzing what wasn't working. I was hard on myself at times, I reminded myself of how it felt when in the moment of shame and lack of self-worth constantly, to never fall into that whirlpool of distractions again. I took up meditation to focus because somewhere I understood it was my mind playing. There was something that needed work there. These remedies worked temporarily, and I was back on track academically. As I was picking myself up academically and ambitiously, my life took a big turn. On one hand, I had my ambitions and on the other the expectations of the society I was living in. This time the expectations pulled me down. My parents had enough money to give me a good wedding or support my higher education. The society around me made me believe there is nothing better than finding a good life partner and having a great wedding. And since there was a marriage proposal perfect on paper, knocking at the door, I should take it. This was a new happening and I was unprepared. I didn't have a sense of judgement as to if it is good or bad. I knew I wasn't ready, but I also wasn't sure enough that things could go wrong when I as a person didn't have a clarity of who I was and where my contentment lies in. Again, lost and uncertain, I picked the expectation over the other factors. Naive and lost, not realizing how important it is to know your self-worth, before inviting another person into your life, I followed my emotions that were smitten by the charm and ended up getting married in early 20s and moved to another country in pure faith that my dreams will be fulfilled by another person, that I can lead a life of emotion and expectations without knowing self-worth. The marriage failed miserably. I wasn't so worried for myself in the moment because somewhere I felt a relief that I didn't have to continue living the pattern of life, that didn't honor my soul. It just wasn't me and I kept saying to myself – this cannot be your life. But at the same time, there was the immense grief of getting the heart broken and leaving someone, you thought was going to share their rest of the life with. It was one of the most difficult choices of my life and I still don't think I made the choice, but the choice was made for me through circumstances. Yet, I always felt a Grace through everything I was going through. A higher hand of someone. As if something was about to turn my life around. It did seem like a faraway truth though, but I believed in it. Perhaps it's a coincidence, divine intervention, whatever one may call it that changed my life around forever, for good. One of the biggest decisions of my life was made in a span of ten minutes on my way to the airport. The plan was to bid goodbye to my loved ones in New York and return to my own country eventually, walking away from the marriage and the life I came with dreams of. The idea to stay back and fight for my rights seemed very painful and tiresome at that time. The chaos that might accompany the court hearings restrained me from fighting for my rights. Disheartened and demotivated I made up my mind to go back to my country and take my life from there. However, I felt devastated for my parents who lead a simple life and only wanted the best for their daughter and now were holding themselves responsible for the marriage, that may have not been the right thing for me at that time. They stood by me now and supported the decisions of my heart. Everything was a blur at that time. People were giving advice from every direction, but nothing seemed to be in resonance with what my heart was wanting. On my way to the airport, we stopped to see a distant relative. Someone I had known from India. We met for a brief span of half hour but before I left, she slipped a small note into my hand. The note had the name of a lawyer and a phone number. I looked at her confused. She didn't say much but glanced at me and said, "Think about it. He is an efficient lawyer." We set off to the airport. I was feeling extremely restless and uneasy by now. We were ten minutes away from the airport, and my restlessness was not getting any better. Finally, the restlessness took over completely and in a moment of anxiety I uttered the words almost involuntarily-"I wish to see this lawyer." And thus began my journey of finding the Self in a foreign land.

    I moved to New York with my uncle and aunt-my second set of parents. They not only took me in, but they also helped me rebuilt my life with all the support they could possibly give. I had a huge support from everyone around me – my brother, family, cousins, extended family and my closest friends. But I was lost. I was unable to figure out what is it that I want from life. Guilt, regrets and lack of self-worth engulfed me completely and no matter how much people were comforting me, I just couldn't come out of it. I cried for months alone in my room staring at walls. I was dying a slow death inside. It was a mourning phase. I had a broken heart and a broken life and to make things worse I was also in the middle of an ongoing immigration case fighting for my survival and a second chance to rebuild my life. There were possibilities and uncertainties. I had to march with the blind faith that the possibilities are going to win over the uncertainties.

Life was asking for a lot of patience from me. It's hard to look back now and see the sequence of changes that came in later that lead me to where I am today. But it was a grace that operated throughout, keeping me safe. My visits to the public library with my aunt were the beginnings of change as far as I remember. I invited myself into the world of books. Reading books, listening to talks, long walks were the beginnings of second episode of introspection. Constructive criticism from some others, also helped me look within. What wasn't working I asked myself and why isn't it working. I understood there was a part of myself that I liked and a part of myself I really didn't. So, my next immediate goal became about changing what I didn't like about myself and to safeguard what I liked about myself. Both needed a lot of hard work. It wasn't easy to do either. A few quotes helped me stay afloat when it came to safeguarding what I liked about myself – "Only speak when asked to and only if it is going to uplift someone". I truly believed in this but often swayed away from it, when triggered emotionally. I took an oath to safeguard it as much as possible. "Always follow your heart"- I was a dreamer and I continued to believe in my dreams, cutting the noise outside. I took an oath to never again mistake expectations to the voice of my Self. The only courage you need is to follow your heart. I decided to safeguard the voice that was always trying to tell me something but, it wasn't until now that I really began hearing it and listening to it. What I disliked about myself was my physical appearance. I wanted to feel tall and healthy and carry the body that I call the temple of my soul, more gracefully. I wanted to eat right, do what's right to keep the body elegant and healthy. I started focusing on healthy foods, tuned into my body, made it a point to get some workout in my daily routine for the rest of my life, at least few times a week. I decided to eat and do what gave me a connection of mind, body and soul. I never followed a particular diet or regime. I did what I found to be meditative. With time I lost the unnecessary weight I had gained and regained the energy I had lost. It also became my source of meditation. Be it walking on a treadmill or going for a run or even long walks. I started fully immersing myself in it, cutting any outer voice and listening to my inner voice that had so much to share. With time, it became a part of me. Like drinking water for survival. There was a current of something wonderful flowing underneath now. Maybe it was always there, and I never saw it. My vision was getting clear now. A year or two are had passed. Circumstantially nothing much has changed. The wait was still on. I was waiting on the immigration to give me a verdict. But I was now feeling a power from within. A power of possibilities. A power to safeguard the voice from within and to follow it, the power to say no, the power to give things time that need time to sprout, the power to work where work is needed without worrying about the result, the power to practice silence, the power to be with the Self, the power to not fear. Yet there was a big lesson yet to be learnt. The art of letting go of an idea I once wanted so bad-the idea of how the marriage should have been. A big power I lacked at this point. Through all this self-transformation a part of me aimed to revive the lost idea of marriage I had in me. It was also the biggest driving force to gather myself, to get it together. There was a bubble yet to broken to reveal the deep purpose behind all that had happened.

With time, the circumstances changed, miracles kept happening one after the other. They probably always did but now I could distinctly see them. From winning the case with immigration, getting admitted to a Pharm D program in Florida, to someone sitting in the Department of Education reading my emails that were crying for help with federal student loans that were stuck because of my pending immigration case until then, and them calling my university to make sure nothing was going stop me from attending the class of 2013, everything was orchestrated beautifully. When I look back now, I am just in the awe of everything that helped me rise to where I am today. Getting the right support from family and friends, first car, first job everything seems seamless now when I look back because the mindset had changed drastically. I was independent and free now. Just the way I always dreamt of from the childhood. Yet there was the regret I needed to get over.

Now starts the second innings of my life. A miracle that enabled me to truly let go, feel whole again and lead me to my current life partner and the life we have together now. I wouldn't have imagined meeting someone like my life partner now if it hadn't been for a higher Grace. I always knew him as a friend of my best friend. There were quite a few misses before we could start dating. The first time we were to be introduced, I was engaged and so my friend never further lead the conversation and I moved to the US with my first marriage. But this is what makes a true believer out of me. I had achieved all that I wished with a lot of grace, hard work and patience. I now felt the freedom to lead a life of choice. Now I had the career and life I was comfortable in. A second marriage was, however, never something I was feeling authentically connected to without finding that authentic connection with someone and it was hard to figure out what I was looking for in a partner because of the overshadow of my first marriage on my mind. I wasn't sure what was the right thing to do-do I wait for the first marriage to fix itself or do I stay the way I am or do I try connecting with someone again. There was still a part of me that hadn't fully recognized the Doer. The plan was already in place. On a devastating day, I get the news of my previous life partner moving on with someone. And I felt the ground underneath my feet shaken. That was the deepest grief I had ever felt in a lifetime. I still remember sitting outside a Chapel, on a rainy evening, where I was attending baptism of a friend's niece, and calling my closest friend, broken hearted. Tears rolling down my cheeks as I tell my friend it's over. At that point, I truly recognized that my idea of how that marriage should have been, was over and although it hurt, I was fully able to recognize the path I had taken to reach where I was, and that now it was time to fully let go of the what the ego anticipated should happen. This was the final closure to the chapter that my heart was holding on to, inhibiting myself from experiencing any connection was someone.

Months past, and my heart started healing. There was a sense of relief. The past year from that, I did come across some wonderful gentlemen-kind, smart, loving and encouraging. But none left an impact like my present husband did. Strangely so, he was the only one I was afraid to get connected to in the past because it felt different with him. And since I didn't have a full closure until then from my previous marriage, I was too afraid to have my heart spilt between two men. After hitting the rock bottom, getting the much-needed closure from the past, the dawn finally came upon me. My heart had opened again. And the first person I wished to connect with was my current life partner. And the rest was history. We got married two years later and what I have now is not just a life partner but everything thing I thought I had lost, with the loss of my first marriage. And this is what tells me there is a higher hand of someone there. To restore every dream I had, after all the twists and turns, wouldn't be possible if

my ego was the one in control. The Doer had to be someone bigger than the ego. What continues now is a journey of possibilities and contentment. Nothing is more valuable to me than the feeling of true contentment. Anything I do now focusses on achieving contentedness and the power to say no to the situations that demand a compromise on my contentment. I am grateful for the journey that the Doer has set me on and it truly feels a little bit like freedom that feels little bit like love that feels a little bit like peace.